cover: "Near Andersonville"
Homer Winslow, 1866
oil on canvas

THE STORY
OF
MATTIE J. JACKSON

as given by Mattie.

written and arranged by
Dr. L. S. Thompson

forward by
Rev. Lewis E. Floyd Jr. MDIV MUM
Third Baptist Church,
Lawrence, Mass.

Afterward by
J. Godsey

SICPRESS 2012
METHUEN, MASS.

The Story of Mattie J. Jackson as written and arranged by Dr. L. S. Thompson, was originally published in Lawrence, Mass. at the Sentinel office, in 1866.

For further research read: *Speaking lives, authoring texts: three African American women's oral slave narratives.* Fulton Minor, DoVeanna S., Reginald H. Pitts, Louisa Picquet, Mattie J. Jackson, and Cornelius Wilson Larison. 2010. Albany: State University of New York Press.

Thank you to Rev. Floyd for his contribution to the publication of this volume.

©2012
series edited by J. Godsey
sales@SicPress.com
Methuen, Mass.

TABLE OF CONTENTS

Forward to the New Edition

This volume is a powerful and enduring piece of writing that we all need to read. What stands out about Mattie Jackson is her sophistication and determination for freedom at all cost. Her story is one of the many untold stories of slavery. Her story touches the human soul as we picture the injustice of black labor and white wealth. Still, we see the strength of a slave woman as she carries on after the separation from siblings and loved ones. The spirit of Mattie Jackson echoes a sense of sadness and joy, sadness regarding her years as a slave, but joy from her determination to escape slavery and complete her education. Joy that she wrote her experiences down, so that others could read and understand her experience.

This tradition of slave writing from oral narration, speaks life into the dead and relates the quiet resistance of complicity; as well as the responsibility for and involvement in, the dreaded past of a torn yet still great nation. A nation, which, in today's world, must still lead and be led by people who feel themselves responsible to never forget how we got from there to here.

Mattie Jackson's Christianity shines clearly through her poetry, not only did it change "the moral aspect of nations." It changed her, and she wrote her story, so that others like me could read and feel, and reflect on the past to move forward and tell our own stories so that other will hear.

Dr. Lewis E. Floyd, Jr.
Lawrence, Mass.

PREFACE

The object in publishing this book is to gain sympathy from the earnest friends of those who have been bound down by a dominant race in circumstances over which they had no control—a butt of ridicule and a mark of oppression; over whom weary ages of degradation have passed. As the links have been broken and the shackles fallen from them through the unwearied efforts of our beloved martyr President Lincoln, as one I feel it a duty to improve the mind, and have ever had a thirst for education to fill that vacuum for which the soul has ever yearned since my earliest remembrance.

Thus I ask you to buy my little book to aid me in obtaining an education, that I may be enabled to do some good in behalf of the elevation of my emancipated brothers and sisters. I have now arrived at the age of twenty. As the first dawn of morning has passed, and the meridian of life is approaching, I know of no other way to speedily gain my object than through the aid and patronage of the friends of humanity.

M.J.J.

NOTE. Miss Jackson sustains a high moral character—has been much respected since she has been in Lawrence. She is from St. Louis, Missouri, and arrived here on the 11th of April, 1866. To gain the wish of the heart is utterly impossible without more means than she can obtain otherwise. Her friends have borne her expenses to Lawrence, and have and are still willing to render her aid as far their limited means will allow. She was in the same condition of all the neglected and oppressed. Her personal requirements are amply supplied. She now only craves the means to clothe and qualify the intellect. My humble prayer is that she may meet with unlimited success.

This young lady is highly worthy of all the aid our kind friends feel a duty to bestow upon her. She purposes lecturing and relating her story; and I trust she may render due satisfaction and bear some humble part in removing doubts indulged by the prejudices against the natural genius and talent of our race. May God give her grace and speed her on her way.

Respectfully yours,

L. S. T.

MATTIE'S STORY.

My ancestors were transported from Africa to America at the time the slave trade flourished in the Eastern States. I cannot give dates, as my progenitors, being slaves, had no means of keeping them. By all accounts my great grandfather was captured and brought from Africa. His original name I never learned. His master's name was Jackson, and he resided in the State of New York. My grandfather was born in the same State, and also remained a slave for some length of time, when he was emancipated, his master presenting him with quite an amount of property. He was true, honest and responsible, and this present was given him as a reward. He was much encouraged by the cheering prospect of better days. A better condition of things now presented itself. As he possessed a large share of confidence, he came to the conclusion, as he was free, that he was capable of selecting his own residence and manage his own affairs with prudence and economy. But, alas, his hopes were soon blighted. More heart rending sorrow and degradation awaited him. He was earnestly invited by a white decoyer to relinquish his former design and accompany him to Missouri and join him in speculation and become wealthy. As partners, they embarked on board a schooner for St. Charles, Mo. On the passage, my grandfather was seized with a fever, and for a while was totally unconscious. When he regained his reason he found himself, near his journey's end, divested of his free papers and all others. On his arrival at St. Charles he was seized by a huge, surly looking slaveholder who claimed him as his property. The contract had previously been concluded by his Judas-like friend, who had received the bounty. Oh, what a sad disappointment. After serving for thirty years to be thrust again into bondage where a deeper degredation and sorrow and hopeless toil were to be his portion for the remaining years of his existence. In deep despair and overwhelmed with grief, he made his escape to the woods, determined to put an end to his sorrows by perishing with cold and hunger. His master immediately pursued him, and in twenty-four hours found him with hands and feet frostbitten, in consequence of which he lost the use of his fingers and toes, and was thenceforth of little use to his new master. He remained with him, however, and married a woman in the same station in life. They lived as happily as their circumstances would permit. As Providence allotted, they only had one son, which was my father, Westly Jackson. He had a deep affection for his family, which the slave ever cherishes for his dear ones. He had no other link to fasten him to the human family but his fervent love for those who were bound to him by love and sympathy in their wrongs and sufferings. My grandfather remained in the same family until his death. My father, Westly Jackson, married, at the age of twenty-two, a girl owned by James Harris, named Ellen Turner. Nothing of importance occurred until three years after their marriage, when her master, Harris failed through the extravagance and mismanagement of his wife, who was a great spendthrift and a dreaded terror to the poor slaves and all others with whom she associated in common circumstances, consequently the entire stock was sold by the sheriff to a trader residing in Virginia. On account of the good reputation my mother sustained as a worthy servant and excellent cook, a tyrannical and much dreaded slaveholder watched for an opportunity to purchase her, but fortunately arrived a few moments too late, and she was bid off in too poor a condition of health to remain long a subject of banter and speculation. Her husband was allowed to carefully lift her down from the block and accompany her to her new master's, Charles Canory, who treated her very kindly while

12

she remained in his family. Mr. Canory resided in St. Charles County for five years after he purchased my mother. During that time my father and mother were in the same neighborhood, but a short distance from each other. But another trial awaited them. Her master removed twenty miles away to a village called Bremen, near St. Louis, Mo. My father, thereafter, visited my mother once a week, walking the distance every Saturday evening and returning on Sunday evening. But through all her trials and deprivations her trust and confidence was in Him who rescued his faithful followers from the fiery furnace and the lion's den, and led Moses through the Red Sea. Her trust and confidence was in Jesus. She relied on His precious promises, and ever found Him a present help in every time of need. Two years after this separation my father was sold and separated from us, but previous to his delivery to his new master he made his escape to a free State. My mother was then left with two children. She had three during the time they were permitted to remain together, and buried one. Their names were Sarah Ann, Mattie Jane and Esther J. When my father left I was about three years of age, yet I can well remember the little kindnesses my father used to bestow upon us, and the deep affection and fondness he manifested for us. I shall never forget the bitter anguish of my parents' hearts, the sighs they uttered or the profusion of tears which coursed down their sable checks. O, what a horrid scene, but he was not her's, for cruel hands had separated them.

The strongest tie of earthly joy that bound the aching heart—
His love was e'er a joyous light that O'er the pathway shone—
A fountain gushing ever new amid life's desert wild—
His slightest word was a sweet tone of music round her heart—
Their lives a streamlet blent in one. O, Father, must they part?
They tore him from her circling arms, her last and fond embrace—

O never again can her sad eyes gaze upon his mournful face.

It is not strange these bitter sighs are constant bursting forth.

Amid mirth and glee and revelry she never took a part,

She was a mother left alone with sorrow in her heart.

But my mother was conscious some time previous of the change that was to take place with my father, and if he was sold in the immediate vicinity he would be likely to be sold again at their will, and she concluded to assist him to make his escape from bondage. Though the parting was painful, it afforded her solace in the contemplation of her husband becoming a free man, and cherishing a hope that her little family, through the aid of some angel of mercy, might be enabled to make their escape also, and meet to part no more on earth. My father came to spend the night with us, according to his usual custom. It was the last time, and sadness brooded upon his brow. It was the only opportunity he had to make his escape without suspicion and detection, as he was immediately to fall into the hands of a new master. He had never been sold from the place of his birth before, and was determined never to be sold again if God would verify his promise. My father was not educated, but was a preacher, and administered the Word of God according to the dictation and revelation of the spirit. His former master had allowed him the privilege of holding meetings in the village within the limits of his pass on the Sundays when he visited my mother. But on this Saturday evening he arrived and gave us all his farewell kiss and hurried away. My mother's people were aware of my father's intention, but rather than spare my mother, and for fear she might be detected, they secreted his escape. His master called a number of times and enquired for him and strongly pressed my mother to give him an account of my father, but she never gave it. We waited patiently, hoping to learn if he succeeded in gaining his freedom. Many anxious weeks and months passed before we could get any tidings from him, until at length my mother heard that he was in Chicago, a free man and preaching the Gospel. He made every effort to get his family, but all in vain. The spirit of slavery so strongly existed that letters could not reach her; they were all destroyed. My parents had never learned the rescuing scheme of the underground railroad which had borne so many thousands to the standard of freedom and victories. They knew no other resource than to depend upon their own chance in running away and secreting themselves. If caught they were in a worse condition than before.

THEIR ATTEMPT TO MAKE
THEIR ESCAPE

Two years after my father's departure, my mother, with her two children, my sister and myself, attempted to make her escape. After traveling two days we reached Illinois. We slept in the woods at night. I believe my mother had food to supply us but fasted herself. But the advertisement had reached there before us, and loafers were already in search of us, and as soon as we were discovered on the brink of the river one of the spies made enquiries respecting her suspicious appearance. She was aware that she was arrested, consequently she gave a true account of herself—that she was in search of her husband. We were then destitute of any articles of clothing excepting our wearing apparel. Mother had become so weary that she was compelled to leave our package of clothing on the way. We were taken back to St. Louis and committed to prison and remained there one week, after which they put us in Linch's trader's yard, where we remained about four weeks. We were then sold to William Lewis. Mr. Lewis was a very severe master, and inflicted such punishment upon us as he thought proper. However, I only remember one severe contest Mr. Lewis had with my mother. For some slight offence Mrs. Lewis became offended and was tartly and loudly reprimanding her, when Mr. L. came in and rashly felled her to the floor with his fist. But his wife was constantly pulling our ears, snapping us with her thimble, rapping us on the head and the sides of it. It appeared impossible to please her. When we first went to Mr. L.'s they had a cowhide which she used to inflict on a little slave girl she previously owned, nearly every night. This was

17

done to learn the little girl to wake early to wait on her children. But my mother was a cook, as I before stated, and was in the habit of roasting meats and toasting bread. As they stinted us for food my mother roasted the cowhide. It was rather poor picking, but it was the last cowhide my mother ever had an opportunity to cook while we remained in his family. Mr. L. soon moved about six miles from the city, and entered in partnership with his brother-in-law. The servants were then divided and distributed in both families. It unfortunately fell to my lot to live with Mrs. Larry, my mistress' sister, which rendered my condition worse than the first. My master even disapproved of my ill treatment and took me to another place; the place my mother resided before my father's escape. After a short time Mr. Lewis again returned to the city. My mother still remained as cook in his family. After six years' absence of my father, my mother married again a man by the name of George Brown, and lived with her second husband about four years, and had two children, when he was sold for requesting a different kind and enough food. His master considered it a great insult, and declared he would sell him. But previous to this insult, as he called it, my step-father was foreman in Mr. L.'s tobacco factory. He was trusty and of good moral habits, and was calculated to bring the highest price in the human market; therefore the excuse to sell him for the above offence was only a plot. The morning this offence occurred, Mr. L. bid my father to remain in the kitchen till he had taken his breakfast. After pulling his ears and slapping his face bade him come to the factory; but instead of going to the factory he went to Canada. Thus my poor mother was again left alone with two more children added to her misery and sorrow to toil on her weary pilgrimage.

Racked with agony and pain she was left alone again,
With a purpose nought could move

And the zeal of woman's love,
Down she knelt in agony
To ask the Lord to clear the way.

True she said O gracious Lord,
True and faithful is thy word;
But the humblest, poorest, may
Eat the crumbs they cast away.

Though nine long years had passed
Without one glimmering light of day
She never did forget to pray
And has not yet though whips and chains are castaway.

For thus said the blessed Lord,
I will verify my word;
By the faith that has not failed,
Thou hast asked and shall prevail.

We remained but a short time at the same residence when
Mr. Lewis moved again to the country. Soon after, my little
brother was taken sick in consequence of being confined in
a box in which my mother was obliged to keep him. If permitted to creep around the floor her mistress thought it would
take too much time to attend to him. He was two years old
and never walked. His limbs were perfectly paralyzed for
want of exercise. We now saw him gradually failing, but was
not allowed to render him due attention. Even the morning
he died she was compelled to attend to her usual work. She
watched over him for three months by night and attended to
her domestic affairs by day. The night previous to his death
we were aware he could not survive through the approaching day, but it made no impression on my mistress until she
came into the kitchen and saw his life fast ebbing away, then

she put on a sad countenance for fear of being exposed, and told my mother to take the child to her room, where he only lived one hour. When she found he was dead she ordered grave clothes to be brought and gave my mother time to bury him. O that morning, that solemn morning. It appears to me that when that little spirit departed as though all heaven rejoiced and angels veiled their faces.

My mother too in concert joined -

Her mingled praise with them combined.

Her little saint had gone to God

Who saved him with his precious blood.

Who said "Suffer little children to come unto me and forbid them not."

The Soldiers, and Our Treatment During the War

Soon after the war commenced the rebel soldiers encamped near Mr. Lewis' residence, and remained there one week. They were then ordered by General Lyons to surrender, but they refused. There were seven thousand Union and seven hundred rebel soldiers. The Union soldiers surrounded the camp and took them and exhibited them through the city and then confined them in prison. I told my mistress that the Union soldiers were coming to take the camp. She replied that it was false, that it was General Kelley coming to re-enforce Gen. Frost. In a few moments the alarm was heard. I told Mrs. L. the Unionists had fired upon the rebels. She replied it was only the salute of Gen. Kelley. At night her husband came home with the news that Camp Jackson was taken and all the soldiers prisoners. Mrs. Lewis asked how the Union soldiers could take seven hundred men when they only numbered the same. Mr. L. replied they had seven thousand. She was much astonished, and cast her eye around to us for fear we might hear her. Her suspicion was correct; there was not a word passed that escaped our listening ears. My mother and myself could read enough to make out the news in the papers. The Union soldiers took much delight in tossing a paper over the fence to us. It aggravated my mistress very much. My mother used to sit up nights and read to keep posted about the war. In a few days my mistress came down to the kitchen again with another bitter complaint that it was a sad affair that the Unionists had taken their delicate citizens who had enlisted and made prisoners of them— that they were babes. My mother reminded her of taking Fort Sumpter and Major Anderson and serving them the same and that turn about was fair play. She then hastened to her room with the speed of a deer, nearly unhinging every door in her flight, replying as she went that the Niggers and Yankees were seeking to take the country. One day, after she had visited the kitchen to superintend some domestic affairs, as she pretended, she became very angry without a word being passed, and said— "I think it has come to a pretty pass, that old Lincoln, with his long legs, an old rail splitter, wishes to put the Niggers on an equality with the whites; that her children should never be on an equal footing with a Nigger. She had rather see them dead." As my mother made no reply to her remarks, she stopped talking, and commenced venting her spite on my companion servant. On one occasion Mr. Lewis searched my mother's room and found a picture of President Lincoln, cut from a newspaper, hanging in her room. He asked her what she was doing with old Lincoln's picture. She replied it was there because she liked it. He then knocked her down three times, and sent her to the trader's yard for a month as punishment. My mistress indulged some hopes till the victory of New Orleans, when she heard the famous Union song sang to the tune of Yankee Doodle:

The rebels swore that New Orleans never should be taken,
But if the Yankees came so near they should not save their bacon.
That's the way they blustered when they thought they were so handy,
But Farragut steamed up one day and gave them Doodle Dandy

Ben Butler then was ordered down to regulate the city;
He made the rebels walk a chalk, and was not that a pity?
That's the way to serve them out——that's the way to treat them,
They must not go and put on airs after we have beat them.

He made the rebel banks shell out and pay the loyal people,

He made them keep the city clean from pig's sty to church steeple.

That's the way Columbia speaks, let all men believe her;

That's the way Columbia speaks instead of yellow fever.

He sent the saucy women up and made them treat us well

He helped the poor and snubbed the rich; they thought he was the devil.

Bully for Ben. Butler, then, they thought he was so handy;

Bully for Ben Butler then,—Yankee Doodle Dandy.

The days of sadness for mistress were days of joy for us. We shouted and laughed to the top of our voices. My mistress was more enraged than ever—nothing pleased her. One evening, after I had attended to my usual duties, and I supposed all was complete, she, in a terrible rage, declared I should be punished that night. I did not know the cause, neither did she. She went immediately and selected a switch. She placed it in the corner of the room to await the return of her husband at night for him to whip me. As I was not pleased with the idea of a whipping I bent the switch in the shape of W, which was the first letter of his name, and after I had attended to the dining room my fellow servant and myself walked away and stopped with an aunt of mine during the night. In the morning we made our way to the Arsenal, but could gain no admission. While we were wandering about seeking protection, the girl's father overtook us and persuaded us to return home. We finally complied. All was quiet. Not a word was spoken respecting our sudden departure. All went on as usual. I was permitted to attend to my work without interruption until three weeks after. One morning I entered Mrs. Lewis' room, and she was in a room adjoining, complaining of something I had neglected. Mr. L. then enquired if I had done my work. I told him I had. She then

23

flew into a rage and told him I was saucy, and to strike me, and he immediately gave me a severe blow with a stick of wood, which inflicted a deep wound upon my head. The blood ran over m clothing, which gave me a frightful appearance. Mr. Lewis then ordered me to change my clothing immediately. As I did not obey be became more enraged, and pulled me into another room and threw me on the floor, placed his knee on my stomach, slapped me on the face and beat me with his fist, and would have punished me more had not my mother interfered. He then told her to go away or he would compel her to, but she remained until he left me. I struggled mightily, and stood him a good test for a while, but he was fast conquering me when my mother came. He was aware my mother could usually defend herself against one man, and both of us would overpower him, so after giving his wife strict orders to take me up stairs and keep me there, he took his carriage and drove away. But she forgot it, as usual. She was highly gratified with my appropriate treatment, as she called it, and retired to her room, leaving me to myself. I then went to my mother and told her I was going away. She bid me go, and added "May the Lord help you." I started for the Arsenal again and succeeded in gaining admittance and seeing the Adjutant. He ordered me to go to another tent, where there was a woman in similar circumstances, cooking. When the General found I was there he sent me to the boarding house. I remained there three weeks, and when I went I wore the same stained clothing as when I was so severely punished, which has left a mark on my head which will ever remind me of my treatment while in slavery. Thanks be to God, though tortured by wrong and goaded by oppression, the hearts that would madden with misery have broken the iron yoke.

MR. LEWIS CALLS AT
THE BOARDING HOUSE

At the expiration of three weeks Mr. Lewis called at my boarding house, accompanied by his brother-in-law, and enquired for me, and the General informed him where I was. He then told me my mother was very anxious for me to come home, and I returned. The General had ordered Mr. Lewis to call at headquarters, when he told him if he had treated me right I would not have been compelled to seek protection of him; that my first appearance was sufficient proof of his cruelty. Mr. L. promised to take me home and treat me kindly. Instead of fulfilling his promise he carried me to the trader's yard, where, to my great surprise, I found my mother. She had been there during my absence, where she was kept for fear she would find me and take my brother and sister and make her escape. There was so much excitement at that time, (1861), by the Union soldiers rendering the fugitives shelter and protection, he was aware that if she applied to them, as he did not fulfill his promise in my case, he would stand a poor chance. If my mother made application to them for protection they would learn that he did not return me home and immediately detect the intrigue. After I was safely secured in the trader's yard, Mr. L. took my mother home. I remained in the yard three months. Near the termination of the time of my confinement I was passing by the office when the cook of the Arsenal saw and recognized me and informed the General that Mr. L. had disobeyed his orders, and had put me in the trader's yard instead of taking me home. The General immediately arrested Mr. L and gave him one hundred lashes with the cow-hide, so that they might identify him by a scarred back, as well as his slaves. My mother had the pleasure of washing his stained clothes, otherwise it would not have been known. My master was compelled to pay three thousand dollars and let me out. He then put me to service, where I remained seven months, after which he came in great haste and took me into the city and put me into the trader's yard again. After he received the punishment he treated my mother and the children worse than ever, which caused her to take her children and secrete themselves in the city, and would have remained undetected had it not been for a traitor who pledged himself to keep the secret. But King Whiskey fired up his brain one evening, and out popped the secret. My mother and sister were consequently taken and committed to the trader's yard. My little brother was then eight years of age, my sister sixteen, and myself eighteen. We remained there two weeks, when a rough looking man, called Capt. Tirrell, came to the yard and enquired for our family. After he had examined us he remarked that we were a fine looking family, and bid us retire. In about two hours he returned, at the edge of the evening, with a covered wagon, and took my mother and brother and sister and left me. My mother refused to go without me, and told him she would raise an alarm. He advised her to remain as quiet as possible. At length she was compelled to go. When she entered the wagon there was a man standing behind with his hands on each side of the wagon to prevent her from making her escape. She sprang to her feet and gave this man a desperate blow, and leaping to the ground she made an alarm. The watchmen came to her assistance immediately, and there was quite a number of Union policemen guarding the city at that time, who rendered her due justice as far as possible. This was before the emancipation proclamation was issued. After she leaped from the wagon they drove on, taking her children to the boat. The police questioned my mother. She told them that Capt. Tirrell had put her children on board the boat, and was going to take them to Memphis and sell them into hard slavery. They accompanied her to the boat, and arrived just as they were casting off. The police ordered them to stop and immediately deliver up the children, who had been secreted in the Captain's private apartment. They were brought forth and returned. Slave speculation was forbidden in St. Louis at that time. The Union soldiers had possession of the city, but their power was limited to the suppression of the selling of slaves to go out of the city. Considerable smuggling was done, however, by pretending Unionism, which was the case with our family.

Released From the Trader's Yard and Taken to Her New Master

Immediately after dinner my mother called for me to accompany her to our new home, the residence of the Captain, together with my brother and sister. We fared very well while we were there. Mrs. Tirrell was insane, and my mother had charge of the house. We remained there four months. The Captain came home only once a week, and he never troubled us for fear we might desert him. His intention was to smuggle us away before the State became free. That was the understanding when he bought us of Mr. Lewis, as it was not much of an object to purchase slaves while the proclamation was pending, and they likely to lose all their property; but they would, for a trifle purchase a whole family of four or five persons to send out of the State. Kentucky paid as much, or more than ever, for slaves. As they pretended to take no part in the rebellion they supposed they would be allowed to keep them without interference. Consequently the Captain's intention was to keep as quiet as possible till the excitement concerning us was over, and he could get us off without detection. Mr. Lewis would rather have disposed of us for nothing than have seen us free. He hated my mother in consequence of her desire for freedom, and her endeavors to teach her children the right way as far as her ability would allow. He also held a charge against her for reading the papers and understanding political affairs. When he found he was to lose his slaves he could not bear the idea of her being free. He thought it too hard, as she had raised so many tempests for him, to see her free and under her own control. He had tantalized her in every possible way to humiliate and

29

annoy her; yet while he could demand her services he appreciated and placed perfect confidence in mother and family. None but a fiendish slaveholder could have rended an honest Christian heart in such a manner as this.

Though it was her sad and weary lot to toil in slavery
But one thing cheered her weary soul
When almost in despair
That she could gain a sure relief in attitude of prayer

Capt. Tirrell Removes the Family—Another Strategy

One day the Captain commenced complaining of the expense of so large a family, and proposed to my mother that we should work out and he take part of the pay. My mother told him she would need what she earned for my little brother's support. Finally the Captain consented, and I was the first to be disposed of. The Captain took me in his buggy and carried me to the Depot, and I was put into a Union family, where I remained five months. Previous to my leaving, however, my mother and the Captain entered into a contract—he agreeing not to sell us, and mother agreeing not to make her escape. While she was carrying out her promise in good faith, he was plotting to separate us. We were all divided except mother and my little brother, who remained together. My sister remained with one of the rebels, but was tolerably treated. We all fared very well; but it was only the calm before the rending tornado. Captain T. was Captain of the boat to Memphis, from which the Union soldiers had rescued us. He commenced as a deck hand on the boat, then attained a higher position, and continued to advance until he became her Captain. At length he came in possession of slaves. Then his accomplishments were complete. He was a very severe slave master. Those mushroom slaveholders are much dreaded, as their severity knows no bounds.

Bondage and torture, scourges and chains
Placed on our backs indelible stains.

I stated previously, in relating a sketch of my mother's history, that she was married twice, and both husbands were to be sold and made their escape. They both gained their freedom. One was living,—the other died before the war. Both made every effort to find us, but to no purpose. It was some years before we got a correct account of her second husband, and he had no account of her, except once he heard that mother and children had perished in the woods while endeavoring to make their escape. In a few years after his arrival in the free States he married again.

When about sixteen years of age, while residing with her original master, my mother became acquainted with a young man, Mr. Adams, residing in a neighboring family, whom she much respected; but he was soon sold, and she lost trace of him entirely, as was the common occurrence with friends and companions though united by the nearest ties. When my mother arrived at Captain Tirrell's, after leaving the boat, in her excitement she scarce observed anything except her little group so miraculously saved from perhaps a final separation in this world. She at length observed that the servant who was waiting to take her to the Captain's residence in the country was the same man with whom she formed the acquaintance when sixteen years old, and they again renewed their acquaintance. He had been married and buried his wife. It appeared that his wife had been in Captain Tirrell's family many years, and he also, for some time. They had a number of children, and Capt. Tirrell had sold them down South. This cruel blow, assisted by severe flogging and other ill treatment, rendered the mother insane, and finally caused her death.

In agony close to her bosom she pressed,

The life of her heart, the child of her breast—

Oh love from its tenderness gathering might

Had strengthed her soul for declining age.

But she is free. Yes, she has gone from the land of the slave;

The hand of oppression must rest in the grave.

The blood hounds have missed the scent of her way,

The hunter is rifled and foiled of his prey.

After my mother had left the Captain to take care of herself and child, according to agreement with the Captain, she became engaged to Mr. Adams. He had bought himself previously for a large price. After they became acquainted, the Captain had an excellent opportunity of carrying out his stratagem. He commenced bestowing charity upon Mr. Adams. As he had purchased himself, and Capt. T. had agreed not to sell my mother, they had decided to marry at an early day. They hired a house in the city and were to commence housekeeping immediately. The Captain made him a number of presents and seemed much pleased with the arrangement. The day previous to the one set for the marriage, while they were setting their house in order, a man called and enquired for a nurse, pretending he wanted one of us. Mother was absent; he said he would call again, but he never came. On Wednesday evening we attended a protracted meeting. After we had returned home and retired, a loud rap was heard at the door. My Aunt enquired who was there. The reply was, "Open the door or I will break it down." In a moment in rushed seven men, four watchmen and three traders, and ordered mother to take my brother and me and follow them, which she hastened to do as fast as possible, but we were not allowed time to put on our usual attire. They thrust us into a close carriage. For fear of my mother alarming the citizens they threw her to the ground and choked her until she was nearly strangled, then pushed her into a coach. The night was dark and dreary; the stars refused to shine, the moon to shed her light.

'Tis not strange the heavenly orbs

In silence blushed 'neath Nature's sable garb

When woman's gagged and rashly torn away

33

Without blemish and without crime.

Unheeded by God's holy word:—

Unloose the fetters, break the chain,

And make my people free again,

And let them breath pure freedom's air

And her rich bounty freely share.

Let Eutopia stretch her bleeding hands abroad;

Her cry of anguish finds redress from God.

We were hurried along the streets. The inhabitants heard our cries and rushed to their doors, but our carriage being perfectly tight and the alarm so sudden, that we were at the jail before they could give us any relief. There were strong Union men and officers in the city, and if they could have been informed of the human smuggling they would have released us. But oh, that horrid, dilapidated prison, with its dim lights and dingy walls, again presented itself to our view. My sister was there first, and we were thrust in and remained there until three o'clock the following afternoon. Could we have notified the police we should have been released, but, no opportunity was given us. It appears that this kidnapping had been in contemplation from the time we were before taken and returned; and Captain Tirrell's kindness to mother,—his benevolence towards Mr. Adams in assisting him to furnish his house,—his generosity in letting us work for ourselves,—his approbation in regard to the contemplated marriage was only a trap. Thus instead of a wedding Thursday evening, we were hurled across the ferry to Albany Court House and to Kentucky through the rain and without our outer garments. My mother had lost her bonnet and shawl in the struggle while being thrust in the coach, consequently she had no protection from the storm, and the rest of us were in similar circumstances. I believe we passed through Springfield. I think it was the first stopping place after we left East St. Louis, and we were put on board the cars and secreted in the gentlemen's smoking car, in which there were only a few rebels. We arrived in Springfield about twelve o'clock at night. When we took the cars it was dark, bleak and cold. It was the 18th of March, and as we were without bonnets and clothing to shield us from the sleet and wind, we suffered intensely. The old trader, for fear that mother might make her escape, carried my brother, nine years of age, from one train to the other. We then took the cars for Albany, and arrived at eight o'clock in the morning. We were then carried on the ferry in a wagon. There was another family in the wagon, in the same condition. We landed at Portland, from thence to Louisville, and were put into John Clark's trader's yard, and sold out separately, except my mother and little brother, who were sold together. Mother remained in the trader'syard two weeks, my sister six, myself four.

THE FARE AT THEIR NEW HOMES

Mother was sold to Captain Plasio, my sister to Benj Board, and myself to Capt. Ephraim Frisbee. The man who bought my mother was a Spaniard. After she had been there a short time he tried to have my mother let my brother stop at his saloon, a very dissipated place; to wait upon his miserable crew, but my mother objected. In spite of her objections he took him down to try him, but some Union soldiers called at the saloon, and noticing that he vas very small, they questioned him, and my brother, child like, divulged the whole matter. The Captain, fearful of being betrayed and losing his property, let him continue with my mother. The Captain paid eight hundred dollars for my mother and brother. We were all sold for extravagant prices. My sister, aged sixteen, was sold for eight hundred and fifty dollars; I was sold for nine hundred dollars. This was in 1863. My mother was cook and fared very well. My sister was sold to a single gentleman, whose intended took charge of her until they were married, after which they took her to her home. She was her waiter, and fared as well as could be expected. I fared worse than either of the family. I was not allowed enough to eat, exposed to the cold, and not allowed through the cold winter to thoroughly warm myself once a month. The house was very large, and I could gain no access to the fire. I was kept constantly at work of the heaviest kind,—compelled to move heavy trunks and boxes,— many times to wash till ten and twelve o'clock at night. There were three deaths in the family while I remained there, and the entire burden was put upon me. I often felt to exclaim as the Children of Israel did:. "O Lord, my burden is greater than I can bear." I was

37

then seventeen years of age. My health has been impaired from that time to the present. I have a severe pain in my side by the slightest over exertion. In the Winter I suffer intensely with cold, and cannot get warm unless in a room heated to eighty degrees. I am infirm and burdened with the influence of slavery, whose impress will ever remain on my mind and body. For six months I tried to make my escape. I used to rise at four o'clock in the morning to find some one to assist me, and at last I succeeded. I was allowed two hours once in two weeks to go and return three miles. I could contrive no other way than to improve one of those opportunities, in which I was finally successful. I became acquainted with some persons who assisted slaves to escape by the underground railroad. They were colored people. I was to pretend going to church, and the man who was to assist and introduce me to the proper parties was to linger on the street opposite the house, and I was to follow at a short distance. On Sunday evening I begged leave to attend church, which was reluctantly granted if I completed all my work, which was no easy task. It appeared as if my mistress used every possible exertion to delay me from church, and I concluded that her old cloven-footed companion had impressed his intentions on her mind. Finally, when I was ready to start, my mistress took a notion to go out to ride, and desired me to dress her little boy, and then get ready for church. Extensive hoops were then worn, and as I had attached my whole wardrobe under mine by a cord around my waist, it required considerable dexterity and no small amount of maneuvering to hide the fact from my mistress. While attending to the child I had managed to stand in one corner of the room, for fear she might come in contact with me, and thus discover that my hoops were not so elastic as they usually are. I endeavored to conceal my excitement by backing and edging very genteelly out of the door. I had nine pieces of clothing thus concealed on my person, and as the string which fastened them was small it caused me considerable discomfort. To my great satisfaction I at last passed into the street, and my master and mistress drove down the street in great haste and were soon out of sight. I saw my guide patiently awaiting me. I followed him at a distance until we arrived at the church, and there met two young ladies, one of whom handed me a pass and told me to follow them at a square's distance. It was now twilight. There was a company of soldiers about to take passage across the ferry, and I followed. I showed my pass, and proceeded up the stairs on the boat. While thus ascending the stairs, the cord which held my bundle of clothing broke, and my feet became entangled in my wardrobe, but by proceeding, the first step released one foot and the next the other. This was observed only by a few soldiers, who were too deeply engaged in their own affairs to interfere with mine. I seated myself in a remote corner of the boat, and in a few moments I landed on free soil for the first time in my life, except when hurled through Albany and Springfield at the time of our capture. I was now under my own control. The cars were waiting in Jefferson City for the passengers for Indianapolis, where we arrived about nine o'clock.

MATTIE IN INDIANAPOLIS—
THE GLORY OF FREEDOM—PRESIDENT
LINCOLN'S REMAINS EXHIBITED

My first business, after my arrival at Indianapolis was to find a boarding place in which I at once succeeded, and in a few hours thereafter was at a place of service of my own choice. I had always been under the yoke of oppression, compelled to submit to its laws, and not allowed to advance a rod from the house, or even out of call, without a severe punishment. Now this constant fear and restless yearning was over. It appeared as though I had emerged into a new world, or had never lived in the old one before. The people I lived with were Unionists, and became immediately interested in teaching and encouraging me in my literary advancement and all other important improvements, which precisely met the natural desires for which my soul had ever yearned since my earliest recollection. I could read a little, but was not allowed to learn in slavery. I was obliged to pay twenty-five cents for every letter written for me. I now began to feel that as I was free I could learn to write, as well as others; consequently Mrs. Harris, the lady with whom I lived, volunteered to assist me. I was soon enabled to write quite a legible hand, which I find a great convenience. I would advise all, young, middle aged or old, in a free country, to learn to read and write. If this little book should fall into the hands of one deficient of the important knowledge of writing I hope they will remember the old maxim:— "Never to old to learn." Manage your own secrets, and divulge them by the silent language of your own pen. Had our blessed President considered it too humiliating to learn in advanced years, our race would yet have remained under the galling yoke of oppression. After I had been with Mrs. Harris seven months, the joyful news came of the surrender of Lee's army and the capture of Richmond.

Whilst the country's hearts were throbbing,
Filled with joy for victories won;
Whilst the stars and stripes were waving
O'er each cottage, ship and dome,
Came upon like winged lightning
Words that turned each joy to dread,
Froze with horror as we listened:
Our beloved chieftain, Lincoln's dead.

War's dark clouds has long held o'er us,
They have rolled their gloomy fold's away,
And all the world is anxious, waiting
For that promised peaceful day.
But that fearful blow inflicted,
Fell on his devoted head,
And from every town and hamlet
Came the cry our Chieftain's dead.

Weep, weep, O bleeding nation
For the patriot spirit fled,
All untold our century's future—
Buried with the silent dead.
God of battles, God of nations to our country send relief
Turn each lamentation into joy whilst we mourn our murdered chief.

On the Saturday after the assassination of the President there was a meeting held on the Common, and a vote taken to have the President's body brought through Indianapolis, for the people to see his dear dead face. The vote was taken by raising the hands, and when the question was put in favor of it a thousand black hands were extended in the air, seemingly higher and more visible than all the rest. Nor were their hands alone raised, for in their deep sorrow and gloom they raised their hearts to God, for well they knew that He, through martyred blood, had made them free. It was some time before the remains reached Indianapolis, as it was near the last of the route. The body was placed in the centre of the hall of the State House, and we marched in by fours, and divided into twos on each side of the casket, and passed directly through the Hall. It was very rainy,—nothing but umbrellas were to be seen in any direction. The multitude were passing in and out from eight o'clock in the morning till four o'clock in the afternoon. His body remained until twelve o'clock in the evening, many distinguished persons visiting it, when amid the booming of cannon, it moved on its way to Springfield, its final resting-place. The death of the President was like an electric shock to my soul. I could not feel convinced of his death until I gazed upon his remains, and heard the last roll of the muffled drum and the farewell boom of the cannon. I was then convinced that though we were left to the tender mercies of God, we were without a leader.

> Gone, gone is our chieftain,
> The tried and the true;
> The grief of our nation the world never knew.
> We mourn as a nation has never yet mourned;
> The foe to our freedom more deeply has scorned.
>
>
> In the height of his glory in manhood's full prime,
> Our country's preserver through darkest of time;
> A merciful being, whose kindness all shared
> Shown mercy to others. Why was he not spared?

The lover of Justice, the friend of the slave,
He struck at oppression and made it a grave;
He spoke for our bond-men, and chain's from them fell,
By making them soldiers they served our land well.

Because he had spoken from sea unto sea
Glad tidings go heavenward, our country is free,
And angels I'm thinking looked down from above,
With sweet smiles approving his great works of love.

His name with the honor forever will live,
And time to his laurels new lustre will give;
He lived so unselfish, so loyal and true,
That his deeds will shine brighter at every view.

Then honor and cherish the name of the brave,
The champion of freedom, the friend to the slave,
The far-sighted statesman who saw a fair end,
When north land and south land one flag shall defend.

Rest, rest, fallen chieftain, thy labors are o'er,
For thee mourns a nation as never before;
Farewell honored chieftain whom millions adore,
Farewell gentle spirit, whom heaven has won.

SISTER LOST— MOTHER'S ESCAPE— MOTHER'S MARRIAGE

In two or three weeks after the body of the President was carried through, my sister made her escape, but by some means we entirely lost trace of her. We heard she was in a free State. In three months my mother also escaped. She rose quite early in the morning, took my little brother, and arrived at my place of service in the afternoon. I was much surprised, and asked my mother how she came there. She could scarcely tell me for weeping, but I soon found out the mystery. After so many long years and so many attempts, for this was her seventh, she at last succeeded, and we were now all free. My mother had been a slave for more than forty-three years, and liberty was very sweet to her. The sound of freedom was music in our ears; the air was pure and fragrant; the genial rays of the glorious sun burst forth with a new lustre upon us, and all creation resounded in responses of praise to the author and creator of him who proclaimed life and freedom to the slave. I was overjoyed with my personal freedom, but the joy at my mother's escape was greater than anything I had ever known. It was a joy that reaches beyond the tide and anchors in the harbor of eternal rest. While in oppression, this eternal life-preserver had continually wafted her toward the land of freedom, which she was confident of gaining, whatever might betide. Our joy that we were permitted to mingle together our earthly bliss in glorious strains of freedom was indescribable. My mother responded with the children of Israel,—"The Lord is my strength and my song. The Lord is a man of war, and the Lord is his name." We left Indianapolis the day after my mother arrived, and took the cars at eleven o'clock the following evening for St. Louis, my native State. We were then free, and instead of being hurried along, bare headed and half naked, through cars and boats, by a brutal master with a bill of sale in his pocket, we were our own, comfortably clothed, and having the true emblems of freedom.

It appeared to me that the city presented an entirely new aspect. The reader will remember that my mother was engaged to be married on the evening after we were kidnapped, and that Mr. Adams, her intended, had prepared the house for the occasion. We now went in search of him. He had moved about five miles into the country. He had carefully preserved his furniture and was patiently awaiting our return. We were gone two years and four months. The clothing and furniture which we had collected were all destroyed. It was over a year after we left St. Louis before we heard from there. We went immediately from the cars to my aunt's, and from there went to Mr. Adams' residence and took him by surprise. They were married in a week after our return. My mother is comfortably situated on a small farm with a kind and affectionate companion, with whom she had formed an early acquaintance, and from whom she had been severed by the ruthless hand of Wrong; but by the divine hand of Justice they were now reunited forever.

Mattie Meets Her Old Master—Goes to Service—Is Sent For by Her Step-Father in Lawrence, Mass.

In a short time I had selected a place of service, and was improving my studies in a small way. The place I engaged was in the family where I was born, where my mother lived when my father Jackson made his escape. Although Mr. Canory's family were always kind to us, I felt a great difference between freedom and slavery. After I had been there a short time my step-father sent for me and my half brother to come to Lawrence. He had been waiting ever since the State was free, hoping to get some account of us. He had been informed, previously, that mother, in trying to make her escape, had perished by the way, and the children also, but he was never satisfied. He was aware that my aunt was permanently in St. Louis, as her master had given her family their freedom twenty years previous. She was formerly owned by Major Howe, harness and leather dealer, yet residing in St. Louis. And long may he live and his good works follow him and his posterity forever. My father well knew the deception of the rebels, and was determined to persevere until he had obtained a satisfactory account of his family. A gentleman moved directly from Lawrence to St. Louis, who made particular enquiries for us, and even called at my aunt's. We then heard directly from my father, and commenced correspondence. He had not heard directly from us since he made his escape, which was nine years. He had never heard of his little son who my mother was compelled by Mrs. Lewis to confine in a box. He was born eight months after he left. As soon as possible after my mother consented to let my little

47

brother go to his father he sent means to assist us to make preparations for our journey to the North. At first he only sent for his little son. My mother was anxious about sending him alone. He was only eleven years old, and perfectly un-used to traveling and had never been away from his mother. Finally my father came to the conclusion that, as my mother had endured such extreme hardships and sufferings during the nine years he was not permitted to participate or render her any assistance that it would afford him much pleasure in sending for us both, bearing our expenses and making us as comfortable as his means would allow. Money was sent us, and our kind friend, Mr. Howe, obtained our tickets and voluntarily assisted us in starting. We left for the North on Monday, April 9th, and arrived, safe and sound, on the 11th. We found my step-father's residence about six o'clock in the evening. He was not expecting us till the next day. Our meet-ing is better imagined than told. I cannot describe it. His little son was only two years old when he left, and I was eleven, and we never expected to meet him again this side of eter-nity. It was Freedom that brought us together. My father was comfortably situated in a nice white cottage, containing some eight rooms, all well furnished, and attached to it was a fine garden. His wife, who is a physician, was absent, but returned on the following day. The people were kind and friendly. They informed me there was no other colored family in the city, but my step-mother was continually crowded with friends and customers without distinction. My step-mother had bur-ied her only son, who returned from the war in a decline. The white friends were all in deep sympathy with them. I felt immediately at home among such kind and friendly people, and have never felt homesick, except when I think of my poor mother's farewell embrace when she accompanied us to the cars. As soon as my step-mother had arrived, and our excitement was over, they commenced calculating upon plac-ing me in the Sabbath school at the church where my mother belonged. On the next Sabbath I accompanied her and joined

48

the Sabbath school, she occupying a side seat about middle way up the house. I was not reminded of my color except by an occasional loafer or the Irish, usually the colored man's enemy. I was never permitted to attend a white church before, or ride in any public conveyance without being placed in a car for the special purpose; and in the street cars we were not permitted to ride at all, either South or West. Here I ride where I please, without the slightest remark, except from the ignorant. Many ask me if I am contented. They can imagine by the above contrast. My brother and myself entered the public school, and found a host of interested friends and formed many dear acquaintances whom I shall never forget. After attending school a month the term closed. I advanced in my studies as fast as could be expected. I never attended school but one month before. I needed more attention than my kind teacher could possibly bestow upon me, encumbered as she was by so many small children. Mother then proposed my entering some select school and placing myself entirely under its discipline and influence. I was much pleased with the idea, but as they had already been to so much expense for me, I could not wish to place them under any heavier contribution. I had previously told my stepmother my story, and how often my own mother had wished she could have it published. I did not imagine she could find time to write and arrange it, but she immediately proposed writing and publishing the entire story, by the sale of which I might obtain the aid towards completing my studies. I am glad I came to the old Bay State, the people of which the rebels hate with an extreme hatred. I found it just such a place as I had imagined by the appearance of the soldiers and the kindness they manifested.

New England, that blessed land,

All in a happy Union band;

They with the needy share their bread

And teach the weak the Word of God.

49

We never heard from my sister Hester, who made her escape from Kentucky, except when she was on the cars, though we have no doubt she succeeded in gaining her freedom.

Summary

On my return to St. Louis I met my old master, Lewis, who strove so hard to sell us away that he might avoid seeing us free, on the street. He was so surprised that before he was aware of it he dropped a bow. My mother met Mrs. Lewis, her old mistress, with a large basket on her arm, trudging to market. It appeared she had lived to see the day when her children had to wait upon themselves, and she likewise. The Yankees had taken possession, and her posterity were on an equality with the black man. Mr. Lewis despised the Irish, and often declared he would board at the hotel before he would employ Irish help, but he now has a dissipated Irish cook. When I was his slave I was obliged to keep away every fly from the table, and not allow one to light on a person. They are now compelled to brush their own flies and dress themselves and children. Mr. Lewis' brother Benjamin was a more severe slave master than the one who owned me. He was a tobacconist and very wealthy. As soon as the war commenced he turned Unionist to save his property. He was very severe in his punishments. He used to extend his victim, fastened to a beam, with hands and feet tied, and inflict from fifty to three hundred lashes, laying their flesh entirely open, then bathe their quivering wounds with brine, and, through his nose, in a slow rebel tone he would tell them "You'd better walk a fair chalk line or else I'll give yer twice as much." His former friends, the guerrillas, were aware he only turned Union to save his cash, and they gave those persons he had abused a large share of his luxury. They then, in the presence of his wife and another distinguished lady, tortured him in a most inhuman manner. For pretending Union-

51

ism they placed him on a table and threatened to dissect him alive if he did not tell them where he kept his gold. He immediately informed them. They then stood him against the house and fired over his head. From that, they changed his position by turning him upside down, and raising him two feet from the floor, letting him dash his head against the floor until his skull was fractured, after which he lingered awhile and finally died. There was a long piece published in the paper respecting his repentance, benevolence, &c. All the slaves who ever lived in his family admit the Lord is able to save to the uttermost. He saved the thief on the cross, and perhaps he saved him.

When I made my escape from slavery I was in a query how I was to raise funds to bear my expenses. I finally came to the conclusion that as the laborer was worthy of his hire, I thought my wages should come from my master's pocket. Accordingly I took twenty-five dollars. After I was safe and had learned to write, I sent him a nice letter, thanking him for the kindness his pocket bestowed to me in time of need. I have never received any answer to it.

When I complete my education, if my life is spared, I shall endeavor to publish further details of our history in another volume from my own pen.

CHRISTIANITY

Christianity is a system claiming God for its author, and the welfare of man for its object. It is a system so uniform, exalted and pure, that the loftiest intellects have acknowledged its influence, and acquiesced in the justness of its claims. Genius has bent from his erratic course to gather fire from her altars, and pathos from the agony of Gethsemane and the sufferings of Calvary. Philosophy and science have paused amid their speculative researches and wonderous revelations, to gain wisdom from her teachings and knowledge from her precepts. Poetry has culled her fairest flowers and wreathed her softest, to bind her Author's "bleeding brow." Music has strung her sweetest lyres and breathed her noblest strains to celebrate His fame; whilst Learning has bent from her lofty heights to bow at the lowly cross. The constant friend of man, she has stood by him in his hour of greatest need. She has cheered the prisoner in his cell, and strengthened the martyr at the stake. She has nerved the frail and sinking heart of woman for high and holy deeds. The worn and weary have rested their fainting heads upon her bosom, and gathered strength from her words and courage from her counsels. She has been the staff of decrepit age, and the joy of manhood in its strength. She has bent over the form of lovely childhood, and suffered it to have a place in the Redeemer's arms. She has stood by the bed of the dying, and unveiled the glories of eternal life; gilding the darkness of the tomb with the glory of the resurrection.

Christianity has changed the moral aspect of nations. Idolatrous temples have crumbled at her touch, and guilt owned its deformity in her presence. The darkest habitations of earth have been irradiated with heavenly light, and the death shriek of immolated victims changed for ascriptions of praise to God and tho Lamb. Envy and Malice have been rebuked by her contented look, and fretful Impatience by her gentle and resigned manner.

At her approach, fetters have been broken, and men have risen redeemed from dust, and freed from chains. Manhood has learned its dignity and worth, its kindred with angels, and alliance to God.

To man, guilty, fallen and degraded man, she shows a fountain drawn from the Redeemer's veins; there she bids him wash and be clean. She points him to "Mount Zion, the city of the living God, to an innumerable company of angels, to the spirits of just men made perfect, and to Jesus the Mediator of the new Covenant," and urges him to rise from the degradation of sin, renew his nature and join with them. She shows a pattern so spotless and holy, so elevated and pure, that he might shrink from it discouraged, did she not bring with her a promise from the lips of Jehovah, that he would give power to the faint, and might to those who have no strength. Learning may bring her ample pages and her ponderous records, rich with the spoils of every age, gathered from every land, and gleaned from every source. Philosophy and science may bring their abstruse researches and wonderous revelations—Literature her elegance, with the toils of the pen, and the labors of the pencil—but they are idle tales compared to the truths of Christianity. They may cultivate the intellect, enlighten the understanding, give scope to the imagination, and refine the sensibilities; but they open not to our dim eyes and longing vision, the land of crystal founts and deathless flowers. Philosophy searches earth; Religion opens heaven. Philosophy doubts and trembles at the portals of eternity; Religion lifts the veil, and shows us golden streets, lit by the Redeemer's countenance, and irradiated by his smile. Philosophy strives to reconcile us to death; Religion triumphs over it. Philosophy treads amid the pathway of stars, and stands a delighted listener to the music of the spheres; but Religion gazes on the glorious palaces of God, while the harpings of the blood-washed, and the songs of the redeemed, fall upon her ravished ear. Philosophy has her place; Religion her important sphere; one is of importance here, the other of infinite and vital importance both here and hereafter.

Amid ancient lore the Word of God stands unique and preeminent. Wonderful in its construction, admirable in its adaptation, it contains truths that a child may comprehend, and mysteries into which angels desire to look. It is in harmony with that adaptation of means to ends which pervades creation, from the polypus tribes, elaborating their coral homes, to man, the wondrous work of God. It forms the brightest link of that glorious chain which unites the humblest work of creation with the throne of the infinite and eternal Jehovah. As light, with its infinite particles and curiously blended colors, is suited to an eye prepared for the alterations of day; as air, with its subtle and invisible essence; is fitted for the delicate organs of respiration; and, in a word, as this material world is adapted to man's physical nature; so the word of eternal truth is adapted to his moral nature and mental constitution. It finds him wounded, sick and suffering, and points him to the balm of Gilead and the Physician of souls. It finds him stained by transgressions and defiled with guilt, and directs him to the "blood that cleanseth from all unrighteousness and sin." It finds him athirst and faint, pining amid the deserts of life, and shows him the wells of salvation and the rivers of life. It addresses itself to his moral and spiritual nature, makes provision for his wants and weaknesses, and meets his yearnings and aspirations. It is adapted to his mind in its earliest stages of progression, and its highest state of intellectuality. It provides light for his darkness, joy for his anguish, a solace for his woes, balm for his wounds, and heaven for his hopes. It unveils the unseen world, and reveals him who is the light of creation, and the joy of the universe, reconciled through the death of His Son. It promises the faithful a blessed re-union in a land undimmed with tears, undarkened by sorrow. It affords a truth for the living and a refuge for the dying. Aided by the Holy Spirit, it guides us through life, points out the shoals, the quicksands and hidden rocks which endanger our path, and at last leaves us with the Eternal God for our refuge, and his everlasting arms for our protection.

Afterward

Mattie J. (Martha Jane) Jackson was born on a plantation in St. Louis, Missouri, second of three daughters of Westley Jackson and Ellen Turner. In 1866, at nineteen years old, she brought her eleven-year-old half-brother, George to Lawrence, Massachusetts to live with his father, John G. Thompson, who after escaping from slavery had changed his name from George Brown. Mattie related her slave experiences to her stepmother, Lucy Susan Prophet Schuyler Thompson, a practitioner of herbalist medicine, who transcribed and published the story to raise funds for Jackson's education. Mattie finished her education in Lawrence, and move back home to St. Louis, to rejoin her mother, Ellen and her sister Hester, with whom she had lost contact when this book was written.

In 1869, Mattie married a Mississippi steam boat porter, William Reed Dyer, from Warrenton, Missouri, moving into their own home in the city of St. Louis. They had eight children, of which only four boys and a girl reached maturity. Their eldest son, William Henry Dyer, worked as an elevator operator at the St. Louis City Hall, he died young leaving a widow and three children. Another son, Arthur Thomas Dyer who worked as a Pullman dining car chef and lived in Denver and Chicago, he married twice with a son from each marriage. Their youngest child, Warren Charles Dyer who, worked on factory assembly lines, his entire life, yet held a U.S. Patent filed in 1922, for an improved back scrubber. Her only daughter, Edith, married an oil field worker and she ran a boardinghouse, after separating from him, she worked as a seamstress, and died of tuberculosis at a young age.

William and Mattie Dyer move to Dardenne, Missouri in 1895, about thirty-five miles from St. Louis, they own real estate in Dardenne and in the neighboring community of O'Fallon, Missouri. Mattie Jackson Dyer died February 5, 1910 in Dardenne, at sixty-three.

Lucy Susan Prophet was born March 15, 1813, in Rutland, Mass., the daughter of a family of African Americans and Native Americans of the Pequod tribe. She most likely learned to read and write in the Rutland schools, and earned her title of "Doctor" as a botanical physician using herbal remedies. Sometime around 1837, she married the Reverend Peter Schuyler, in Worcester, Mass., an itinerant preacher in the African Methodist Episcopal Church. He died in 1850 and of their seven children, only her youngest son, Arthur Thomas, reached maturity.

Dr. Schuyler is a conductor on the Underground Railroad and is involved in a number of court cases involving runaway slaves, in Worcester and in Lawrence, where she and her son moved in 1855. During this time, she met George Brown, an escaped slave from St. Louis, who was working as a barber in a local hotel. They married Dr. Schuyler in 1860, and settled into a house at 292 Common Street; for some time, she advertised her treatments and medicines in the local newspapers.

Arthur T Schuyler, who was only 15, falsified his age and enlisted in Company C of the 54th Massachusetts Infantry, on March 4, 1863. He served through the war, including the battle of Fort Wagner. When he returned home in

September 1865, he was already suffering from tuberculosis, and died the following April.

Lucy Thompson died in Lawrence, Massachusetts on March 20, 1881 at sixty-eight years and five days. John G. Thompson would died in 1882.

INDEX